D0119757

£3.40

WELCOME TO....

THE BEEZER BOOK

Printed and Published in Great Britain by D. C. Thomson & Co., Ltd.,
185 Fleet Street, London EC4A 2HS.
© D. C. THOMSON & CO., LTD., 1990
ISBN 0-85116-480-3

The NUMSKULLS

And —

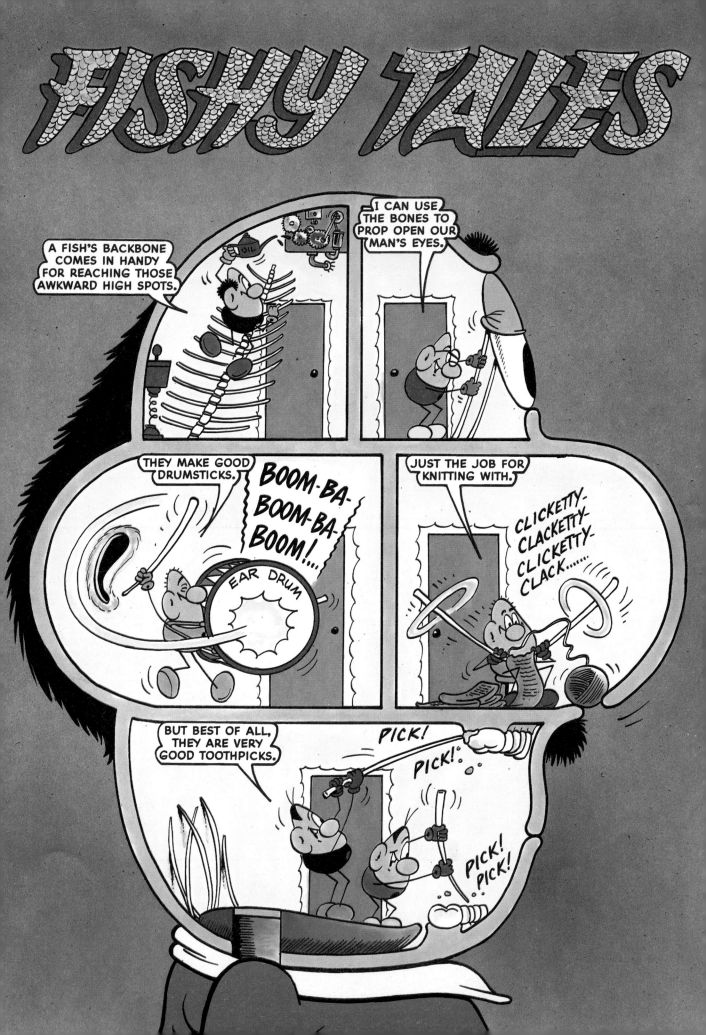

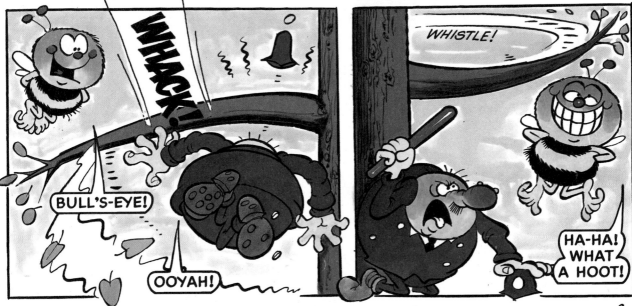

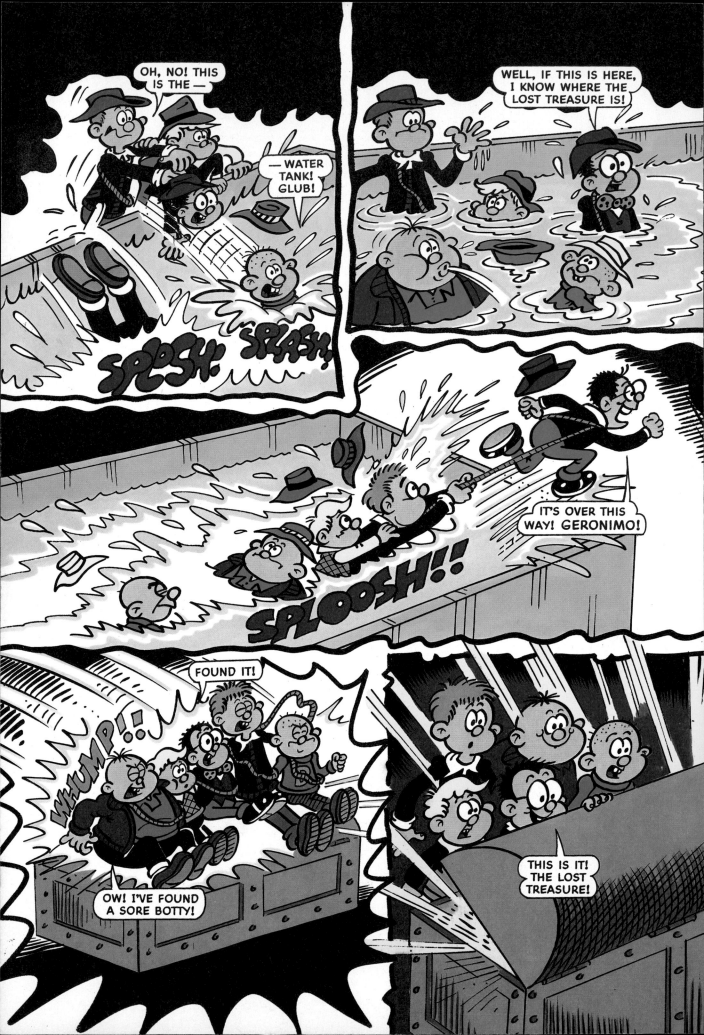

me paint timathy but
he walked over my picture

me stayed up to draw
an owl but me
fell asleep before me
got finished

Me paint froot but me got hungry

me loves Motor racin'

A bowl of Flowers. me had to run — STING was having Din Dins —

Pictures by Baby Crockett

MY DAD — he doesn't Like it — wonder why?

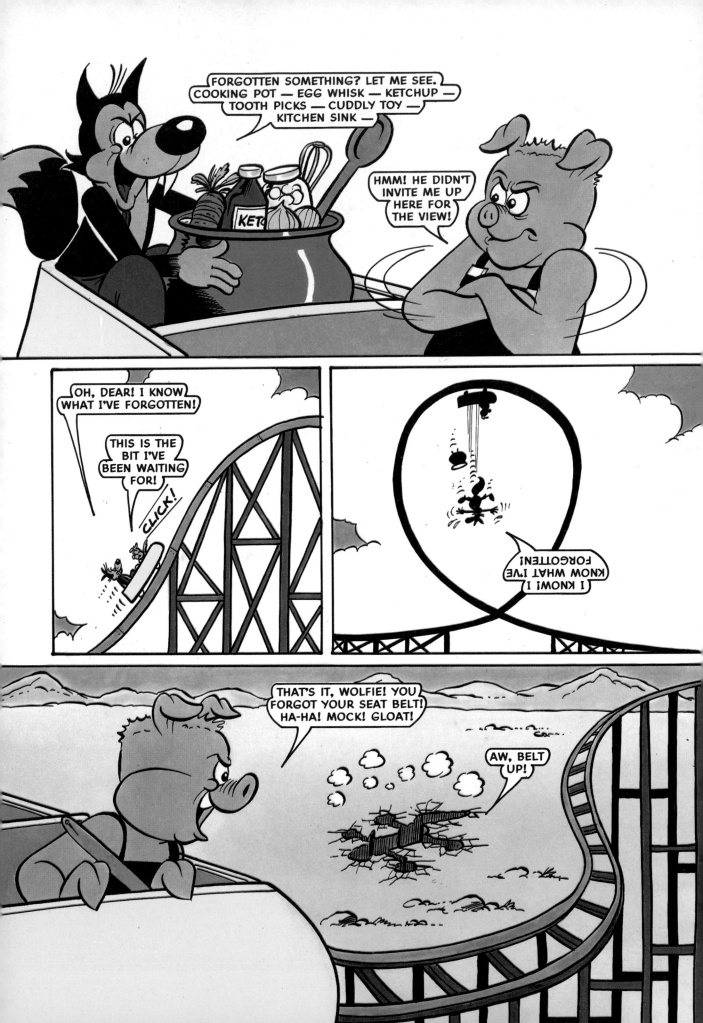

C

THE BADD LADS

COURT IN THE ACT!

NO, LADS, WE'RE GOING TO A LAW COURT, NOT A TENNIS COURT!

OH, DEAR!

OH, DEAR, OH, DEAR!

HA-HA-HA! I'M YOUR LAWYER AND YOU'VE NO CHANCE! YOU'RE GUILTY! HA-HA-HA! HA-HA-HA-HO!

CHARMING, I'M SURE!

WELL, IF THAT'S HOW YOU FEEL, WE SHALL CONDUCT OUR DEFENCE!

WHOO-HA-HA! EVEN FUNNIER! HA-HA! HO-HO! HEE-HEE-HEE!

BUT WE CAN'T EVEN CONDUCT A BAND, BOSS!

TRUE!

PYWARP!

THE RESCUE OF BETTY THE YETI

Late one night in the Beezer building, a lone artist is hard at work —

I'VE INVENTED A NEW COMIC CHARACTER. HOPE THE EDITOR LIKES IT!

BEEZER ROOM

WHAT'S THIS? BETTY THE YETI? SHE'S TOO SOPPY TO USE IN THE BEEZER BOOK!

SIGH! I BET THE READERS WOULD HAVE LIKED BETTY THE YETI! STILL — BACK TO THE OLD DRAWING BOARD!

SNIFF! GOODBYE FOR EVER, BETTY!

PAM and SCRATCHER

DINNER-TIME!

WAYEY! GRUB UP!

GANGWAY.

FROM NOW ON IT'S HEALTH FOOD FOR YOU.

CHEESE? YUK! MOUSE FOOD.

I'LL EAT THE BOWL INSTEAD.

LOB

IT'S HEALTH FOOD FOR YOU TWO, AS WELL.

A SALAD? THRILLING, I DON'T THINK.

HUMPH!

I'D DO ANYTHING TO MISS SCHOOL TODAY!

SAFARI PARK.

HMM! THAT BABY GORILLA DOESN'T LOOK TOO HAPPY WITH LIFE EITHER!

LET'S SWAP PLACES, CHUM...

HAR! HAR! THE GORILLA'S OFF TO SCHOOL IN MY PLACE!

I'LL GIVE MISS GRIMME SOME FLOWERS AND SHE WON'T BOTHER ABOUT MY HOMEWORK.

Suddenly —
LEAVE MY LUPINS ALONE!
OW!

OOH! THAT'S A NASTY WIND THAT'S SUDDENLY SPRUNG UP.
HUH! MISS GRIMME WILL PUT THE WIND UP ME WHEN I TELL HER ABOUT NOT DOING MY HOMEWORK.
ISN'T IT?

Suddenly —
OOMPH!
WHUMP!

WHEE! I'LL GIVE THESE ARTIFICIAL FLOWERS TO MISS GRIMME. SHE WON'T KNOW THE DIFFERENCE.

Later —
HERE SHE COMES NOW!

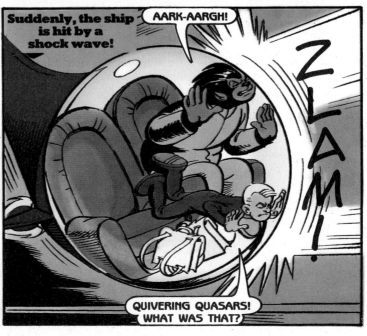

BLINKY AGED SIX MONTHS. HE WAS ALWAYS PLAYING WITH TEDDY BEARS.

AT SCHOOL, BLINKY KEPT IN WITH TEACHER BY BRINGING HIM APPLES.

IN TIME, BLINKY DID GET TO LIKE INDIAN TEA.

BLINKY GAVE UP ASTRONOMY BEFORE TOO LONG.

DESPITE A BAD START IN THE ARMY, BLINKY WENT ON TO BECOME A COLONEL.

WHILST IN AFRICA, BLINKY REGULARLY ENJOYED A GAME OF POLO.

HE DIDN'T LAST LONG AT SKIING, EITHER.

AND HERE HE IS TODAY, IN A TYPICAL POSE.

Yes, readers. It's time for a punch up.

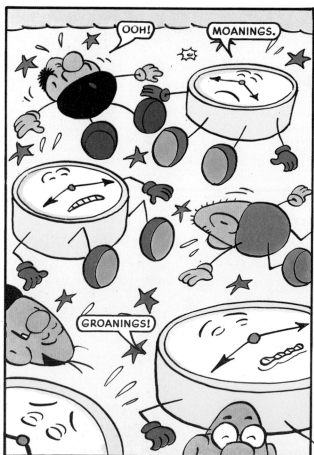